DANCE OF CREATION

*Celtic Prayers of Celebration and Insight,
Repentance and Restoration*

Copyright © 2023, Anamchara Books.

All rights reserved. No part of this publication may be reproduced or transmitted for commercial purposes, except for brief quotations, without written permission of the publisher. Churches and other noncommercial interests may reproduce portions of this book without the express written permission of Anamchara Books, provided that the text does not exceed 500 words or 5 percent of the entire book, whichever is less, and that the text is not material quoted from another publisher. When reproducing text from this book, include the following credit line: "From *Dance of Creation: Celtic Prayers of Celebration and Insight, Repentance and Restoration*, published by Anamchara Books. Used by permission."

Anamchara Books

Vestal, New York 13850

www.AnamcharaBooks.com

Paperback ISBN: 978-1-62524-860-2

eBook ISBN: 978-1-62524-861-9

Celtic ornaments © Arkadii Ivanchenko (Dreamstime.com)

DANCE OF CREATION

*Celtic Prayers of Celebration and Insight,
Repentance and Restoration*

RAY SIMPSON

INTRODUCTION

The Earth is the source of our physical life. In practical, literal terms, we could not live without her. At the same time, she is a source of our spiritual life as well, for God comes to us through Earth's water and light and air, through all things green, through furred and feathered things, and through fungus, microbe, and mineral.

And yet our planet is in trouble. Without a massive revolution in the way we live our lives, Earth faces an ever-advancing crisis. As Ray Simpson reminded us in one of his blog posts, "even churches use non-eco heating, fail to re-wild their churchyards, don't promote local food sharing or teach the biblical truths about creation-care." Ray went on to say: "From start to finish the Scriptures teach that we reap what we sow. The Bible starts with the story of the human lust to take control of earth: the blood spilt by Cain's lust to control makes the earth sterile (Genesis 4:8–12). The Gospels end with an earthquake and the sun's eclipse caused by humans killing the Son of God through whom all creation gets its life (Matthew 27:45–52; John 1:3). The prophets repeatedly point out that human mistreatment makes the earth sterile: "Because everyone ... is greedy and deals falsely (Jeremiah 8:10) the mountains and pastures are laid waste" (9:10); "the earth will become a wasteland because there is no one who cares" (12:11).

In the prayers collected in this book, Ray asks us to "hear the cry of the earth and work together to 'choose life'" (Deuteronomy 30:19). At the same time, he reminds us that the same God who "danced in the morning when the world was young ... in the moon, and the stars, and the sun" (in the words of Sydney Carter's hymn) still dances in all Creation. We are not alone as we face the devastation of our planet, for the Creator longs to work through human minds, ingenuity, commitment, cooperation, and dexterity. "They cut me down," wrote Carter, speaking of Jesus, but he might also have been describing the Earth. "But I leapt up high."

May the promise of Carter's hymn also be true for our planet. Divine life courses through Earth's rivers, breathes through her winds, and sings in each life form she nourishes; may that life leap high again in triumphant joy. And may the prayers in this book teach us to celebrate Earth's beauty as we learn from her deep wisdom. May we repent of our selfishness and ignorance, and commit ourselves to the Earth's healing and restoration, as we participate in the ongoing dance of Creation.

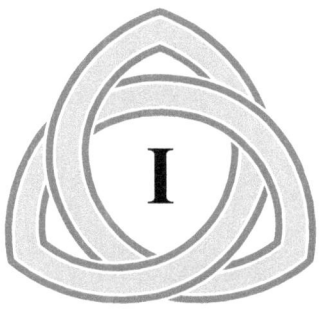

CELEBRATION OF CREATION'S BEAUTY

Maker of all creatures, we honour You.
Friend of all creatures, we honour You.
Life force of all creatures, we honour You.

Earth, whose seeds and fields and food
grow beauty, strength, and mystery,
you bestow to us the finest of your yield,
and we are grateful.
Earth, whose waters, common to all,
flow faithfully through the nights and days,
may you pour on us the milk of your kindness
that brings us lustre.

Divine Birther,
may the whole world celebrate Your existence.
May every person—
each gender, each ability,
each color of skin, and each shape of body—
add colour to the celebration of Your creation.
May every soul join with the song Nature sings.
May the birds sing,
may the trees clap,
and may we humans taste and dance.

The grace of Your creation
is like a cool day
in the midst of summer heat.
We drink in Your creation
with our eyes and with our ears.
How strong and good and sure
Your earth smells.
It is the scent of Your creation;
we drink it in
and cannot get enough of it.
When one day this wonderful world fades
and our bodies' eyes snap shut,
Your beauty will still endure.

(Echoes a prayer from the Ashanti, Ghana.)

Great Creator of the gleaming moon
and falling stars;
Great Saviour of the miraculous birth
and rising from death;
Great Spirit of the seers
and sacred words:
come into our minds,
come into our mouths,
until we become Your message and sign.
Teach us to celebrate the beauty of Your creation
with truth and honor and justice.

Glorious Source, we give You greeting!
Let Sister Earth and Brother Sun praise You.
Let the fields and the forests praise You.
Let the birds and the beasts praise You.
Let everything that has breath praise You,
for you are both the Mother and the Father
of all that has being.

Infinite Birther,
thank You for moments of grace
in the unfolding life of the cosmos:
for the explosion of a star
and the creation of our solar system;
for the cooling aeons and the birth of our planet;
for the seed of life and the emergence of plants;
for the evolution of creatures
and the dawning of human consciousness;
for our ability to make a fire,
a wheel, and a computer.
But far more than these all
we thank You for Yourself
and we celebrate Your Creation.

God bless the earth that is beneath us,

the sky that is above us,

the life that lies before us,

and Your image deep within us.

(Echoes a traditional Scottish blessing.)

May the blessing of the rain be on us,
the sweet soft rain.
May it fall upon our spirits
so that all the little flowers may spring up
and shed their sweetness on the air.
May the blessing of the great rains be upon us,
that they beat upon our spirits
and wash them fair and clean
and leave there many a shining pool
where the blue of heaven shines,
and sometimes a star.

(Echoes a traditional Irish blessing.)

May the freshness and fragrance of the fields
be with us as even on city streets.
May the freshness and fragrance of Your presence
linger with us as we journey on.

You who put beam in golden sun,
You who put food in grain and herd,
You who put fish in stream and sea,
put a grateful heart in us
so we may celebrate Your world.

The food which we are to eat
is earth, water, and sun
coming to us through pleasing plants.
The food which we are to eat
is the fruit of the lives and labour
of many creatures.
We are thankful for it.
May it give us health, strength, and joy;
and may it increase our love.

(Echoes a Unitarian prayer.)

The food that we eat comes to us
through the labours of our Sister Earth,
her creatures,
and our brothers and sisters
far and near.
May we be thankful for this gift.
May we be nourished by the planet's generosity.

Here
may the Earth be full of health,
may the plants be full of goodness,
may the flowers be full of colour,
may the birds be full of song,
may the pets be full of wags,
may the people be full of joy.

We give You thanks for great moments of grace
in the evolution of the cosmos:
for the death of a star
which brought to birth planet Earth.
For the emergence of minerals,
vegetables, and animals.
For the cooperation,
and not just the competition,
between all that lives.
We give thanks for the moments of grace
in the life of a person:
the power of attraction and the wonder of a birth;
for the human person,
endowed with conscience, awe, and intelligence,
a co-creator with You.

Thank You,
Creator of the world,
for the music and medicine of flowers,
which give us a scent of heaven upon earth.
May those who look at them see Your glory
and sing aloud with joy.

Creator of our land,
our earth, the trees,
the animals and humans:
all Creation gives You honour
and sings Your song of joy.

O Monarch of the Tree of Life,
may the blossoms bring forth the sweetest fruit,
may the birds sing out the highest praise,
may Your Spirit's gentle breath cover all,
and may we see and celebrate Your love
that breathes through all life.

We arise today in the promise of the rising seed.
We arise today in the goodness of Creation's life.
With fresh shoots and buds of promise,
may we be glad in the God of life.
With first ears of corn and winged arrivals,
may we be glad in the God of life.

For the beauty and bounty of the world,
its seasons and its gifts;
for the wonder of life
and the Earth on which we live:
we offer You our heartfelt praise.
Unto You, O Lord, be praise
for every flower that ever grew,
every bird that ever flew,
every wind that ever blew.
Unto You, O Lord, be praise
for every flake of virgin snow,
every place where new things grow.
Unto You, O Lord, be praise
for every life that shall be born,
every heart that shall be torn,
every day and every dawn,
every dream and every song,
every joy and every woe,

every friend and every foe.
For the bounty of the world,
unto You, O Lord, be praise.

(Echoes an early Irish prayer.)

The sun rides high and long,
a sign of blessing from our God.
Everything that breathes cries, "Yes!"
At day's fading, may we also
cry, "Yes" to Christ,
the eternal Sun.

The Sun of suns is singing:
Jesus is Lord.
Earth comes to the sun's King:
Jesus is Lord.
Sky comes to the sun's King:
Jesus is Lord.
Spirits come to sun's King, singing:
Jesus is Lord.
Birther, Saviour,
lighting Spirit,
You are the Lord of Light,
the Source of Joy.

Sun shines,

sap rises,

buds burst,

lambs frolic,

birds sing,

people play.

Glory to God

who sustains

and nurtures us all.

God of the rising green,
God of the sweeping blue,
God of the long bright day,
may we, too, give glory to You.
God, eternally awake,
may Your energies flow through us.
God of the rising sap,
may we be Your sap today,
flowing through the Earth,
carrying Your green, life-giving energy
to all that is.

We thank You, Divine Radiance,
for these amazing days;
for the leaping greenery
and the arching blue sky.
Everything that breathes cries, "Yes!"
May our whole being shout back our answer:
"Yes!"

Rejoice, you Earth of sunlit days,
pointing us to Christ, the Sun of rays.
Rejoice, you spirits of earth and air,
saluting Christ on heaven's stair.
Rejoice, you folk in darkened thrall:
Christ scatters darkness, and shines on all.

God of the long day,
You who are eternally awake,
Your energy flowing out like song,
I offer You my eternal *yes,*
the flower of my humanity
the energy and awareness of my days,
the creativity of my life,
the beauty of all Earth's forms,
and the hope of future potential.
God of the long day,
may our lives be long days lit by You,
always reflecting Your light,
open and awake.

Bountiful God,
seed-time has ripened into harvest,
The Earth has yielded fruits.
Winter's cleansing cold
gave way to spring's gentle warmth,
and now summer's full sun has offered us autumn gifts.
With each turning of our planet,
we savour Your presence
with grateful hearts.

God of goodness,
the wonders of Your creation,
the splendour of the heavens,
and the order and richness of Nature
speak to us of Your glory.
The coming of Your Son,
the presence of Your Spirit,
and the fellowship of Your people
show us the marvel of Your love.
The patterns of the year,
the beauty of the Earth,
and the ripening gifts of harvest
call us to worship and adore You.
Hear our heartfelt voices as we cry:
"Yes."
"Amen."

Thank You for harvest's boundless store,
and the fruits of the Earth
that sustain and gladden us.
Thank You for those who work the land,
for each part of the food chain
that reaches to our door.
Thank You for comforts of life
and the power to help others.
Thank You for Your creation
and the life that sings in our blood.

May this season of mellow fruitfulness
enrich and bless us.
May we harvest relationships of trust,
forgiveness, and generosity.
May we be kept in the hollow of God's hand,
and may we sing out loud
the song of harvest home.

Thank You for a roof over our head,
for firm earth under our tread,
for supplies to fill our hunger,
for friends to assuage our anger.
Thank You for all You created,
for the richness of beauty and life.
May our every breath
celebrate Your glory.

Learning from the Wisdom of Creation

As Moon circles Earth,
and the oceans respond
with the rhythms of the tide,
may we too learn to circle You
and reflect back Your rhythms in our lives.

Deep peace of the green-blue sea,
deep peace of the rising sun,
deep peace of the shoreside Christ,
deep peace of the Risen One
be ours today.
Deep peace of the warming sun;
deep peace of the pure white moon;
deep peace of the shining stars;
deep peace of the cleansing winds;
deep peace of the quiet earth;
deep peace of the knowing stones;
deep peace of the forgiving heart.

Deep peace.

Deep peace of the still waters,
deep peace of the setting sun,
deep peace of the forgiving heart,
deep peace of the true call,

deep peace of the Son of Peace
be ours, today, forever.
Deep peace of the Spirit;
peace of the air flowing out to us;
peace of the Son growing strong in us.

(Echoes a prayer of Fiona McLeod.)

As fish live in water, may we live in You.
As birds soar high and carefree,
may we soar with You.
As deer run straight and graceful,
may we run with You.
As water flows so freely,
may we flow with You.

Earth-Maker God,
as the hand is made for holding
and the eyes for seeing,
You have fashioned us for joy.
Grant us Your vision
that we may learn joy from everything—
from the sunlit beauties of our world,
from the wild flower's shy color,
from the lark's melody,
from a child's smile,
from the faces of honest men,
and the strength of loving women.
And may we learn
from each lovely aspect of Creation
that we were made for joy.

Make us attentive
to the lap of the waves, Life-Giver,
and to the movements of the sky,
to the grasses that grow,
and to the soul's every sigh.
Sharpen our vision so we truly see
the landscape beyond our windows,
new scapes coming in,
and the constant mystery of the Earth.
May we sense
the breath of the Spirit in every breeze.
Make us aware of Your precious heartbeats
in the world around us
and in the flow of our own blood.
Open our eyes
and our minds
so that we can see and hear,
learn and love.

RAY SIMPSON

God of Creation,
make us aware of Your presence
in every cell of plant and beast,
and in every cell of our being.
May we listen and learn.

In the flavour of a fruit,
in the flowing of a stream,
in the beauty of a sunset,
may we know that You are good.
In the tossing of the leaves,
in the footsteps of a stag,
in the quiet of the night,
may we learn to hear Your voice.

You who put beam in moon and sun,
You who put fish in stream and sea,
You who put food in grain and herd,
send Your blessing up to us
through every blade and bud
that pushes through the soil.
Bring forth the warmth, the tears, the laughter
from our repressed and frozen ground;
bring forth loving, healing, forgiving
to our fretting, festering wound.
May the Earth teach us what we need to know.
And may we be willing to learn.

Craftsperson of the heavens,
You have stretched out above us
a canopy of stars,
signs of hope renewed in darkest times.
Brightener of the night,
open to us the treasures of darkness:
its deepest wisdom and its healing power.
May we learn from Nature's night
that light is always near.

There is no plant in the ground
but it is full of Your virtue,
O King of the virtues.
May these plants bring Your blessing to us.
There is no life on the Earth
but it proclaims Your goodness,
O King of goodness.
May we learn generosity and cooperation
from all that lives and grows.

May we be real like the elements.
May we be true like the fire.
May we be free like the wind.
May the love that is within us flow like water.
And may we not forget
the sheer, profligate beauty
of the flowers.
Dear God,
give us fragrance in our relationships.

Divine Fashioner of Forms,
we trace Your footprints
in coral reefs and choral music,
in ancient fossils and modern festivals,
in mountain torrents and satellite towers,
in ocean waves and wireless transmissions.
All things work together for good.
How wonderful are Your works.

Lord, You are our island;
in Your bosom we rest.
You are the calm of the sea;
in that peace we stay.
You are the deep waves
of the shining ocean;
with their eternal sound we sing.
You are the song of the birds;
in that tune is our joy.
You are the smooth white sand of the shore;
in You is no gloom.
You are the breaking of the waves on the rock;
Your praise is echoed in the swell.
You are the Lord of our lives;
in You we dwell.

(Echoes a prayer attributed to Saint Columba.)

Bathe us in Your cleansing rivers.
Soak us in Your healing waters.
Drench us in Your powerful downfalls.
Cool us in Your bracing baths.
Refresh us in Your sparkling streams.
Master us in Your mighty seas.
Calm us by Your quiet pools.
Teach us to love
as we rest in Your Creation.

Earth, teach us stillness.
Earth, teach us humility.
May we allow ourselves
to be softened by rain,
dug deep by Providence,
planted with Wisdom's seeds,
replenished by rest,
and made into a hospitable bed
that offers comfort to others.

Give us the eye of the eagle
that gazes into Your face,
traces the movements of Your hand,
penetrates the depths of Your heart,
scans the reaches of Your mind,
and glimpses the horizons of Your Spirit.

Source of Creativity,

teach us

to dance with the playful clouds

and to laugh with the glinting sun.

Teach us

to flow like the sparkling streams

and to soar like the high-winged birds.

Teach us

to dream of rainbow and mountain

and to attempt what we see.

Teach us

to restock memory's treasure-house

and to give it all away.

Lord, may the swirling storm clouds
remind me I am a creature,
not Creator.
I am liable to suffer
from the changes and chances
of this mortal life.
My life, like the clouds,
is ever changing.
May the clouds teach me
to look always to You
the Creator of both storm and sunshine.
May they teach me
to find joy when life is clouded
and to maintain a sense of perspective,
knowing Your love and wisdom,
O Lord, are ever constant.

We go forward in the light of sun,
in the strength of earth,
in the flow of water.
We go forth with the desert hermits
and the holy martyrs,
with all the holy and risen ones.
We go forth with the word of the apostles
and the wisdom of the seers,
with the angels above,
and the prayers of all God's people.
We go forth with each creature,
each tree, each blade of grass;
together, we sing Your song.

May we be as free as the wind,
as soft as sheep's wool,
as straight as an arrow,
that we may journey ever nearer
to the heart of God.

Great Spirit, the birds sing:
what song do You wish to awake
in our hearts?
The clouds open:
what do You wish to open
in our hearts?
The stones know:
what do You wish us to know
in our minds?
The plants come into bloom:
what do You wish to bring to flower
in our time?

The face of Nature laughs in the springtime;
restore laughter to our lives.
Nature's breath is fresh,
and her eyes are clearest blue;
restore freshness to our lives.
The call of the birds is wild and free;
restore liberty to our lives.
Waterfalls splash with joy;
restore joy to our lives.
Meadows light up with flowers;
restore colour to our lives.
The breeze is Nature's harp,
playing a song of love;
restore love-songs to our lives.
The world is in love with its Creator;
restore passion and beauty to our lives.

The sheaves and the green leaves fall;
may our lives be just as generous,
just as ready to surrender.
Open be our hands,
justice be our benchmark,
and thanksgiving be our call.
For the sake of Your great giving,
O Christ who was ground like flour,
our Bread of Life,
to feed and nourish us evermore,
may we too be willing to be spent
like autumn leaves and sheaves,
so that all shall be fed.

The seed is Christ's,
the granary is Christ's.
In the granary of God,
may we be gathered.
The sea is Christ's,
the fishes are Christ's.
In the nets of God
may we all meet.

Harvester God,
as autumn light ripens the grain,
ripen too our souls.
As brown leaves fall
and sheaves are stored,
help us to leave behind summer's ways
and go forward
in deepening compassion,
thankful to heaven
and to Earth.

Great Spirit,
bring to harvest the fragments of our lives
and crown our year with goodness.
Penetrate the storehouse of our memories,
making them whole and holy.
May we, like the Earth, be fruitful.

O sacred season of autumn,
be our teacher,
for we wish to learn
the virtue of contentment.
As we gaze upon your full-coloured beauty
we sense all in you an at-home-ness
with your amber riches.
You are the season of retirement,
of full barns and harvested fields.
The cycle of growth has ceased
and the busy work of giving life
is now completed.
We sense in you no regrets;
for you have lived a full life.
May we learn from your example.

Lord of the elements,
give us a good journey through life.
Lord of the Star of the East,
give us a kindly birth.
Lord of the Star of the South,
give us a great love.
Lord of the Star of the West,
give us a quiet age.
Lord of the Star of the North,
give us a blest death.
Stars and galaxies and infinite space,
teach us the quiet patience of your mystery.

Sun, you gave light to our ancestors.
Moon, you gave comfort to our ancestors.
Air, you gave breath to our ancestors.
Earth, you gave food to our ancestors.
Water, you gave life to our ancestors.
The Earth connects us to a chain of life.
Creator of moon and sun, air, earth, and water,
it was You who gave our ancestors their being.
From You they came;
to You they returned.
Glory to You.

When volcanic ash prevents air flights,
when tsunamis wash away villages,
and when earthquakes obliterate buildings,
teach us that all our agendas
and our achievements are in Your hands.
Let us be schooled by the Earth
and humbled to learn from those around us.

As the trees are stripped of foliage,
may we be stripped of clutter.
As the leaves fall to the ground,
may we fall into Your lap.
As the crops are gathered for harvest,
may the wisdom of our days be garnered.

Star-Kindler,
be our light in the cold and darkness.
Weaver of Wonder,
weave in us the patterns of the winter.
Gatherer of souls,
encompass those we see no longer.
Rock of our salvation,
when winter's cold looms large
and icy winds blow hard,
be our warmth and firm foundation.
We draw near to You,
Creator of stars and snow and winter cold,
with our hearts open to Your love
and our minds ready to learn.

We arise today
in the deep formation of winter,
in the transforming power of ice,
in the cleansing work of frost.
We arise today
in the simplicity of the bare earth,
in the strength of the fierce elements,
in the beauty and brilliance of snow.
Stripped of inessentials,
we stand, rooted in You,
in the anticipation of gathering strength,
for You sustain our well-being.
In the stillness of the bare earth,
we invite You to do Your work in us.

We bind to ourselves this day
    the strength of rock,
    the silence of earth,
    the sharpness of cold.
We bind to ourselves this day
    the longevity of stars,
    the integrity of sky,
    the sobering of dark.

Creating and sustaining God,
as this cold, dark season encroaches,
give to us the stability of the deep earth
and the hope of bright heaven.

REPENTANCE FOR THE HARM WE HAVE DONE OUR WORLD

*Let there be
respect for the Earth,
peace for its people, love in our lives,
delight in the beauty of sky and sea and soil,
forgiveness for past wrongs,
and from now on a new start.*

We confess these sins
that mar Earth's life:
(list them in the silence of your heart).
We call to mind these wild places
and areas rich with Nature's life
that we have neglected:
(list them in silence).
We remember these unjust deeds
we have inflicted on the Earth:
(list them in silence).
We consider these integrities
that have been violated,
both in Nature and in the human world:
(list them in silence).
Show us what can be restored
and the places where we may begin.

You made the Earth,
and through the long ages
planted it with every kind of plant;
You made animals to crawl
and to run upon it,
birds to fly over it
and fish to swim through its waters.
When all was prepared,
You formed humankind from the soil.
You breathed Your life into them.
May we never forget
that we are mortal creatures;
from earth we come, to earth we go.
We did not make ourselves.
We and the Earth
need to be redeemed
through the Saviour
who restores unity

between earth and heaven.
Saviour, bless and redeem us.
Forgive us for the harm
we have done Your world.

Creator of the land,
out of wet mud You fashioned
a wonderful world.
But now we trample upon
and destroy it.
Teach us
to drink in Your love
through Creation,
to shop and eat in grateful awareness
of Your providence,
and to tend the world with care.

Creator and Saviour,
we have exploited Earth
for our selfish ends,
turned our backs on the cycles of life,
and forgotten we are Your stewards.
Now soils become barren,
air and water are sullied,
species disappear,
and humans are diminished.
In penitence we come to You.

Forgive us, Sustainer of Life,
for the polluting waste
dumped by rich nations
on lands of the poor;
for the lust of the privileged
to own and control life forms;
for new forms of colonialism
toward people of color,
as well as women and children,
plants, and animals.
Forgive us, Just One,
for turning Your gifts of water,
ore, oil, and life itself
into products for gain;
for turning the sowing of seed
from a sacred duty
into something forgotten and ignored.

Forgive us, Life-Giver,
for the destruction of biodiversity,
the abundant variety of life
we took for granted,
never realizing we cannot live without it.
Forgive us, God of Love,
for our cruelty,
our selfishness,
and our ignorance.

Creator,
we have raped
and spoiled Your world:
forgive us.
Saviour,
we have ignored Your warnings
to tend the Earth
like a vineyard:
forgive us.
Sustainer,
we have tried to live
as though we had no need
for the Earth
or for You:
forgive us.

You are the Rock
from which all earth is fashioned;
may we recognize
the worth of precious Earth.
You are the Food
from which all life is fed;
may we recognize
the bounty of precious Earth.
You are the Source
from which all matter is forged;
may we recognize
that matter is precious.

Birther,
the planet is in pain.
We have harmed it again and again,
and now it is falling apart.
It is becoming deluged
with pollution
and the rising tides of climate change.
You do not want this,
so we come close to You.
Show us what to stop doing.
Show us what to start doing.
Show us how to build together
a Noah's ark
that's big enough
for our entire planet.

For the rain forests gone,
and the deserts created
by human destruction,
for polluted seas and dirty streets
for not being content to savour
the simple gifts of Creation,
we grieve with You, O God.

WORKING TO RESTORE THE EARTH

Peace to the land and all that grows on it.
Peace to the sea and all that swims in it.
Peace to the air and all that flies through it.
Peace with our God
who calls us to serve and restore the Earth.

Great Provider,
may we receive what the Earth gives us
in respect, in simplicity, in solidarity;
with humility and joy.
May we respond with service
and vocation
to restore the planet we share,
which has given us so much.

You pulled the continents out of the sea.
Out of wet mud
You fashioned hills and plains,
and what beautiful creatures!
We ask Your help not to spoil it.

Nurturing God,
bless this soil,
the soil on which we live and work
and make community.
In Your mercy,
may we learn to bring forth goodness
to nourish and renew
the whole community
of insect and bird, tree and flower,
and human life
who share this soil.

Birther,
make seeds fertile,
make thoughts fruitful,
make waste places flourish.

Renewing God,
Spring has leapt into our midst:
may we spring into action with the same energy
to defend and save Your world.
Let Your seeds sprout in us,
so that we become
restorers, defenders,
protectors of the planet.
Sweep away the cobwebs from our awareness,
and let the innate beauty
with which You dignified our souls
be profligate.

Dear planet,
the Light of all lights shines on you;
the Power of all powers energizes you;
the Love of all loves shelters you.
May you become aware
in each rock and mountain,
each farm and city,
each forest and field,
that the Eternal Three
cares without ceasing
for all forms, all realities.
The One-in-Three ever expresses
with graces, energies,
and creative manifestations.
Dear planet,
may you be healed
from the wounds of human egotism.

May consciousness of the Unity-in-Trinity
dawn upon you.
May cooperation with the One-in-Three
develop upon you.
May you move forward
into your divine destiny.

Holy Spirit,
breathe upon the cosmos.
May it share in Christ's resurrection
and grow with the birth pangs of his kingdom.
May we, even in the middle
of its groanings and agony,
be instruments of its healing
and breathe peace upon it this day.

As the sun circles the world,
circle this land, O God.
Circle the soil, circle the waters.
Circle the crops, circle the homes.
Keep harm without, keep good within.

Life-Giver:
bring buds to flower,
bring rain to the earth,
bring songs to our hearts.
Renewer:
may gardens become green,
may beauty emerge,
may dreams come to pass.

Creator,
You caused the Earth
to bring forth the Saviour.
Spirit, come now
and renew the face of the Earth:
all that grows on it,
all who live on it.
May we participate
in Your healing work.

We offer You the Earth
and the vegetables that grow from it,
for all Creation is Yours,
and we want to be enriching it,
not abusing it.
We offer You the Earth
and the minerals that lie within it,
for all Creation is Yours,
and we want to be enriching it,
not exploiting it.
We offer You the Earth
and the birds and beasts that live upon it;
for all Creation is Yours,
and we want to be enriching it,
not betraying it.
We offer You ourselves
who make our home upon this Earth,
for all Creation is Yours,
and we want to be enriching it.

Dear Planet Earth,
may the Light of all light shine on you,
may the Power of all power energize you,
may the Love of all love transform you.
Dear people of our planet,
may the Love of all love transform you.

Generosity of God,
spilling over into Creation,
flow into Your people
that we may bless the air and the animals.
Teach us to tend the Earth with care,
to give love to Your Creation,
and to live a rhythm that restores
well-being to the planet.

Generosity of God,
spilling over into Creation,
we thank You for flowers
and their wealth of beauty,
for creatures and their glorious variety,
for seas and seasons and scents;
may we, too, reflect
Your boundless generosity.

Dear Saviour,
who restored unity
between earth and heaven,
teach us to care for the Earth
and to be good stewards
of all that is in it.
May our eyes be open
to see Your hand in Nature.
May our hands be open
to cherish Your gifts
in the material things
we reap from the Earth.
May we learn how to live in harmony
with Your laws of love and respect.
Bless the soil
on which we live and work
and make community.
May it bring forth goodness
to nourish and renew all who share it.

Great Spirit,
whose breath is in the soft breeze,
may we cherish the precious Earth,
the Earth of the God of life.
May we provide for those
who can neither sow nor reap
because human ills have drained them.
May we seek always to use the Earth's bounty
only to bless,
and never to satisfy
our selfishness.

Creator,
make us co-workers with You
that the Earth and all who live upon it
may reap a full harvest.
Show us how to reflect Your rhythms
in our life and work.
Teach us to conserve
the world's rich resources,
that we may sustain
a living environment
that sings with well-being
for all life upon the Earth.

Caring Father God,
we offer You the fuels and forests,
the seas and soil,
the air and animals,
the technology and the textiles,
all the treasure of our planet.
May we steward Your creation
to Your glory
and for the benefit
of future generations.

May we love You
by loving the Earth,
every grain of sand.
May we love You in Your skies
and in every ray of light.
May we love You in the animals
and in everything that breathes.
May we love You in Your plants
and in every leaf that greens.
May we love You in Your creation
and in the symphony of the whole.
May we love You for Yourself
and in Your infinite Being
spread out around us.

This we know:
the Earth does not belong to us.
The Earth is God's
and so are all living things.
This we know:
we did not weave the web of life.
The Earth is God's
and so is all that breathes on it.
Whatever befalls the Earth
befalls the daughters and sons of Earth.
The Earth is God's,
and we are called to serve it.

In dependence on the God of life,
may we cherish the precious Earth,
the Earth of the God of life,
the Earth of the Christ of love,
the Earth of the Spirit Holy.
In dependence on the God of life,
may the Earth become our bed of hope.

We bless You, Life-Giver,
for Your covenant with Noah;
renew our relationship with the Earth.
We bless You, Living One,
for Your covenant with Moses;
renew our relationship with the human world.
We bless You, Lord of Life,
for Your covenant with David;
renew our relationship
with those who share our lives.
We bless You, Lover of all life,
for Your covenant with Jesus;
renew our relationship with You.

God bless the oil
and the good things
it has made possible.
God forgive us for grabbing it
and wasting it without wisdom.
God help us
as we reap the harvest
of our misdeeds.
God guide us
as we seek to harness
the cleaner energies
of sun and wind and water.
Make us wise enough, we pray,
to save our planet
and ourselves
from destruction.

We pray
for the well-being of Creation,
the health of the air,
the richness of the Earth,
with all its bounty,
and the beauty of the whole world.

Help us to know, Life-Giver,
that the Earth does not belong to us,
for we belong to Earth.
Help us to know, Living One,
that we did not weave the web of life;
we are merely a strand in it.
Help us to know, Source of all life,
that whatever we do to ourselves,
we do to the Earth.
Help us to know, Spirit of Wisdom,
that whatever befalls the Earth
befalls us as well.

Creator God,
help us to give all creatures
their due respect.
Teach us how to conserve,
to share, to enjoy,
to tend the Earth with care,
to develop agriculture that truly enhances,
to guide science
along wise and considerate ways,
to restore the lands that have been ravaged
until we, the Earth, and You
blossom into a new relationship
of love.

We bring to You,
Healer of our souls:
unvisited places that have no name for love;
abandoned places that lie untended;
stunted places that long to grow again;
resentful places that await forgiving touch;
fearful places that need Your comfort;
defeated places where fresh belief can come;
and polluted places where human selfishness
has left its stamp.
Send us out into these wounded places,
carrying the healing energy,
the practical wisdom,
and the tireless love
of Your Spirit.

Help us,
God of the whole created world,
to buy wisely,
use energy carefully,
travel prayerfully,
eat mindfully,
and exchange thoughtfully.

Divine Restorer, aid us
in regulating our affairs in harmony
with the simple beauty of Creation.
May our belongings, activities, and relationships
be ordered in a way that liberates Spirit.
May our clothes and furniture reflect
God-given features of our personalities,
rather than the desires of our egos.
May we give You our income,
savings, and possessions,
conscious that we are stewards,
rather than owners.

Our society is ever restless,
always craving one more thing to do,
seeking happiness
through more and more possessions.
Teach us to be at peace
with what we have;
to embrace
what we have been given
and received;
to know that enough is enough,
until our strivings cease
and we rest content in You alone.

Help us to follow You
in strength of Trinity,
living by scripture's guidance,
in soul friends' confidence,
in life's rhythms,
in overcoming prayer,
in simplicity of life,
in stewardship of Creation,
in the healing of the world,
in the stream of God's Spirit,
in solidarity with others,
in sharing with all.

(Echoes the Community of Aidan and Hilda vows.)

God of both Monday and Sunday,
You have created a world
of limited natural resources;
and You have created humans
of limited duration and energy.
May we accept our limitations.
May we stop trying to be God.
May we live in a balance
of input and output.

You who are Heroic Love,
alive in every leaf and lane,
beckon us through star and stone
to stride beyond our petty ways.
Lead us in pursuit
of the Endless Adventure
to which You have called us,
the Adventure of love,
of healing and restoration,
of cooperation and forgiveness.

Lord of Earth and Heaven,
remind us:
that the food we eat is truly
earth, water, and air,
coming to us in the form
of plants and creatures.
With each bite we put into our mouths,
remind us:
to be grateful
and to keep it simple.

Help us pluck out by the roots
Adam's sinful greed in Eden
that proved so deadly to the world.
Help us to touch the tree of the cross
that pours out immortality on the world,
that we may flow
with the new river from Paradise
by which all things are made alive.

We pray to You
for this place of desecration:
bring forth beauty from it.
We pray to You
for this hard and barren place:
bring forth generosity from it.
We pray to You
for the greed- and guilt-laden places:
bring forth forgiveness from them
and let eternal life bloom.

We will journey into the Earth's wild places;
with You, we shall neither faint nor fear.
The wild creatures shall become our friends;
with You, we shall neither faint nor fear,
for their Creator also created us.
With You, we shall neither fear nor faint
as we face the consequences of our greed
written across the face of the Earth,
for You are the Creator
who still works to build, to heal, to restore,
and make all things new.
Give glory to the God of heaven and earth.
Give glory to God who fills our world.
We kneel before You,
asking that You fill us with Your love and strength
so that we can partner with You
in the Earth's restoration;
with You, we shall neither faint nor fear.

Bless the Moon that is above us;
the Earth that is beneath us;
the hard work to be done here;
the seedlings that shall grow here;
the neighbours we shall greet here;
and all who live
in the network of life here.

THE PRESENCE OF GOD
IN SEA, EARTH, AND SKY

Glory to the Birther,
glory to the Son,
glory to the Spirit,
who makes creation one.

God, You dance with Creation;
we see Your likeness
in tree and creature,
in sky and sea,
and in stone and star.
Strike the world with thunder
of Your Spirit's Presence;
give us ears to hear and eyes to see,
as You fill the world with love.

God of the elements,
glory to You,
for being our radar in the ocean wide.
Your hand be on our rudder.
Your love be over the mast
on the heaving foam.

High King of land and sea,
wherever we go is Yours.
You led our forebears by cloud and fire.
You lead us through the days and nights.
You led Saint Brendan by sign and sail.
Your Presence goes before us now.
We see You in earth and sky,
wind and rain,
sun and shadow.

For the glory of Creation
ever streaming from Your heart,
we praise You.
For the air of the eternal
seeping through the physical,
we praise You.
For the everlasting glory
dipping into time,
we praise You.
For the wonder of Your presence
beckoning from each leaf,
we praise You.
For setting us,
like the stars in their courses,
within the orbit of Your love,
we praise You.

Glory to You,
the vital Force that vibrates
throughout the cosmos.
Glory to You, the infinite Mind
that understands the cosmos.
Glory to You, the fertile Birther
that conceives each element of the cosmos.
Glory to You, the purest Love
that comes to live with us
in one small corner of the cosmos.
Glory to You, the Gatherer
of planets and peoples, space and time,
the Climax of the cosmos.

There is no plant in the ground
that does not tell of Your beauty, Lord.
May soil and microbe,
tree, pond, fungus, and insect,
and every furred and feathered things
exhale the fragrance of Your love.
May the fruits of the Earth
speak to us of Your mercy,
and may we inhale Your Presence
each time we see the sky.

High-borne eagles and nesting birds,
you are God's friends on Earth.
Speckled trout and mountain deer,
you speak without words God's praise.
Snarling wolf and savage boar
lie down at sainted feet.
Serpents of fear and fierce desire
uncoil and concede defeat.
Creatures tame and creatures wild,
show to us a living God.

Great Spirit,
You nod and beckon to us
through every stone and star.
Your life surges towards us
in every greening leaf.
We hear You in the quiet ripple of slow rivers
and in the thunder of storm-tossed waves.
We are touched by Your beauty
in bird-wing and blossom.
We come to You.

In the chill of wintry wind,
in the depths of uncertain thoughts,
sing to us the story of the universe.
Visit us,
Saviour of our being,
in starlight and cloud,
blizzard and ice.
Teach us to always see
Your face.

Star-Kindler
and Weaver of Wonder,
as winter stars light up
the darkness of night,
reveal to us
fresh sources of hope.
Hold us,
O God of the cold, dark days,
secure in the knowledge
that from its wintry depths
the earth brings forth a Saviour.
Creator God,
whose power and beauty
are never spent,
in wintry earth awaken us
to the mystery of Your presence.

Thank You for leading us
to the time of briefest light
secure in the trust
that You embrace the encircling gloom.
Held by the dark,
which You encompass in Your arms,
we are content to rest in You
like a baby in the womb.

The world is not dead,
it is sleeping.
Its life draws in,
it is keeping.
The Earth is gathering energy
for a new burst of life.
We breathe in the mystic air
that we may breathe out care.
Your Presence supports us through the night
so we can hail the coming source of Light.
Shine through the mists,
the deadening heavy clod,
gladdening Light of Christ our Lord.

Creator of Love,
make us aware that You are present
in every cell of creation
and in every cell of our being.
May we hear You
in the movements of the sky
and in the soul's every sigh.
May we hear You
in the silent wings of a butterfly
and in a frightened creature's cry.
When our pets race and dart,
may we catch the beatings of Your heart.

Lord of the seasons,
on these days of briefest light
help us to be at home
with the treasures of the dark.
As the days have drawn in,
draw near to us
with Your everlasting light.
As shadows lengthen,
help us to embrace
the shadow side of life,
knowing You are here as well.
As the dark swallows up
the created sun,
help us to store up riches
for the long days ahead.
Remind us that the dark is not evil,
for it holds the treasures of Your love.

We bless You, God,
for the goodness of this day.
In the strength of the elephant,
we see Your might;
in the speed of a gazelle,
we see Your flight;
in the suppleness of a fish,
we see Your agility;
in the force of the wind,
we sense Your ability;
on the wings of a bird, we see You fly;
and in the presence of Creation,
we feel You nigh.
The joy of the Earth has its source in You,
for You are the warmth of the sun.
The wreath of Your love circles the Earth,
and the world shines
with the gold of life everlasting.

RAY SIMPSON

Mellow moon, sheen of the night,
your gentle gift to us—
the presence of the silent Spirit—
calms us under your faithful watch.
Bathe us in your quiet light,
that we may be washed in the Spirit.
Encompass us
in the mystery of your light,
that we may sense
the wonder of the unseen.
You, Creator,
who give us this moonlight,
descend through the night's thick clouds
on every child on Earth,
and rest on us.

More books on Celtic spirituality that are also by Ray Simpson . . .

(All are available from Anamchara Books. Amazon, and most online booksellers.)

Celtic Christianity
Deep Roots for a Modern Faith

Celtic Spirituality for the Modern World

The world of the long-ago Celts appeals to many of us in the twenty-first century. Whether we are looking to find our cultural heritage or are seeking an alternative to worn and restrictive religious forms, the earth-centered, woman-friendly, inclusive faith of the Christian Celts offers us a deep-rooted alternative approach to traditional Christianity. The Celts experienced "thin places," where they sensed the supernatural world; they honored their poets, singers, and artists; and they passionately followed the Christ of the Gospels. Theirs was a church without walls, which lived naturally and comfortably within the community. Ray Simpson has spent most of his life walking in the footsteps of the Christian Celts, and now he allows us to experience for ourselves their dynamic spirituality.

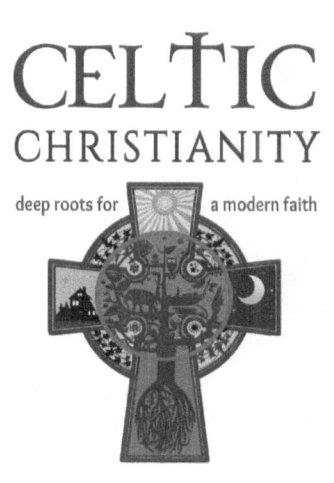

Tree of Life
Celtic Prayers to the Universal Christ

Christ is the visible image of the invisible God. He existed before anything was created and is supreme over all creation, for through him God created everything. . . . He existed before anything else, and he holds all creation together.
—*Colossians 1:15–17*

Like a vast, ever-growing Tree of Life, Christ—the expression of Divine love—expands endlessly throughout the universe. This is the perspective of ancient Celtic spirituality, and it is this concept that Ray Simpson reveals in his poem-prayers. Inspired by the traditional Celtic style of prayer, he gives words to our individual relationships with God. He speaks of the wonder, beauty, and love revealed through the Universal Christ, the Tree of Life that includes all that is. Each and everything in creation is sacred, for everything is a word of God—and we too are called to be God's words to our world.

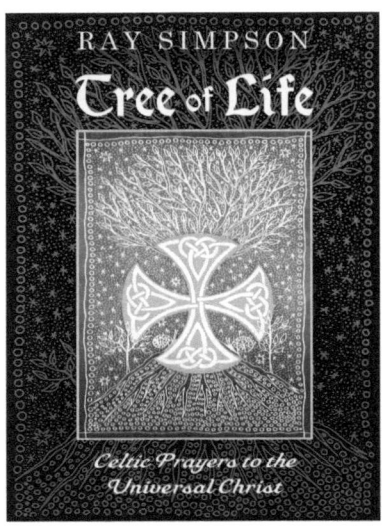

Celtic Prayers for the Rhythm of Each Day

**Every hour is holy,
every day is sacred**

We sometimes think prayer belongs only in certain places on certain days. This book calls us to set prayer free from these constraints, allowing it to flow out through the hours of every workday, sanctifying the ordinary rhythm of our modern lives.

Ray Simpson gives us twenty original prayers, written in the Celtic tradition or patterned after ancient Celtic prayers, for each interval of the day. Like generations of earlier followers of Christ,

we too can use prayer to bless the rhythm of our daily lives, infusing the hours with the awareness of the One who gives us Life. These small pauses throughout the day will make us ever more aware that the Kingdom of Heaven is a constant and present reality, hidden just beneath the veil of everyday life.

The Celtic Book of Days

*Ancient Wisdom for Each Day
of the Year from the
Celtic Followers of Christ*

**This book will change
the way you look at everyday life.**

The ancient Celts found God's presence in each ordinary moment of the day. Everything they encountered revealed to them the presence of the sacred; each day was deep with meaning. Now you too can practice the Celts' faith, as you take a few moments to immerse yourself in their wisdom. These small daily moments of reflection and insight will open your heart to each day and all it holds.

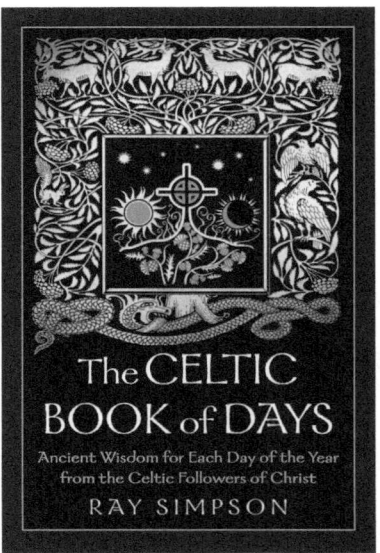

Soul Friendship in the Celtic Tradition

Ancient Insights for Today

The special friend who accompanies a person through life's journey is more precious than gold. The early Christian Celts had a heartwarming name for this person: the Anamchara. (Anam is the Gaelic word for soul; chara is the word for friend—"friend of the soul.") This special friend was someone with whom a person could talk through practical matters, reveal hidden intimacies, and break through the barriers of convention and egotism to an eternal unity of soul.

Ray Simpson brings this ancient concept into the twenty-first century, drawing practical applications from the long history of soul friendship. He describes a spiritual bond that lasts beyond this life into eternity, for it flows directly from God, who is the pattern of all friendship, the center and source of all human relationships.

AnamcharaBooks.com

www.ingramcontent.com/pod-product-compliance
Lightning Source LLC
Chambersburg PA
CBHW060526080526
44586CB00012B/640